Su[...] of

Things That Matter
Charles Krauthammer

Conversation Starters

By Paul Adams
Book Habits

MW00941816

Please Note: This is an unofficial Conversation Starters guide. If you have not yet read the original work, you can purchase the original book here.

Copyright © 2018 by BookHabits. All Rights Reserved. First Published in the United States of America 2018

We hope you enjoy this complementary guide from BookHabits. Our mission is to aid readers and reading groups with quality, thought provoking material to in the discovery and discussions on some of today's favorite books.

Disclaimer / Terms of Use: This guide is unofficial and unauthorized. It is not authorized, approved, licensed, or endorsed by the original book's author or publisher and any of their licensees or affiliates. Product names, logos, brands, and other trademarks featured or referred to within this publication are the property of their respective trademark holders and are not affiliated with BookHabits. The publisher and author make no representations or warranties with respect to the accuracy or completeness of these contents and disclaim all warranties such as warranties of fitness for a particular purpose.

No part of this publication may be reproduced or retransmitted, electronic or mechanical, without the written permission of the publisher.

Bonus Downloads
*Get Free Books with **Any Purchase** of* Conversation Starters!

Every purchase comes with a FREE download!

Add spice to any conversation
Never run out of things to say
Spend time with those you love

Get it Now

or Click Here.

Scan Your Phone

Tips for Using Conversation Starters:

EVERY GOOD BOOK CONTAINS A WORLD FAR DEEPER THAN the surface of its pages. Questions herein are designed to bring us beneath the surface of the page and invite us into the world that lives on. These questions can be used to:

- Foster a deeper understanding of the book
- Promote an atmosphere of discussion for groups
- Assist in the study of the book, either individually or corporately
- Explore unseen realms of the book as never seen before

Table of Contents

Introducing *Things That Matter*

Everyone who has heard the name Krauthammer instantly knows of his journalistic articles as his conservative views on politics. Though born in Montreal and once a staunch member of the Democratic society, Krauthammer soon became a leader amongst conservative intellectuals with his column in the newspaper. While one would normally find his articles in the *Washington Post* as well as countless others, readers can now find his numerous articles in one book for them to easily review and remember. Many of Krauthammer's articles cover important topics central for anyone who wants to see a people as a union shine in their country. His ideas on free markets to keep the prices in the power of the consumers, lower taxes so that we are able to hold more of our hard earned money instead of paying for lavish vacations the country's leaders take, limited government and stronger individual rights are a pleasure to read about. Krauthammer also writes about his views on having a powerful position on foreign policy as well as how this country should fight in its war in terrorism. His articles can be enjoyed by any who are concerned about the direction the country is currently heading with its current senate and cabinet. While some may think that they won't be able to find a common ground with Krauthammer's views, they may be surprised. He has articles in his book about him being pro-choice when it comes to women getting abortions, stating that since it is their body that will carry the fetus for nine months and care for it for the rest of its life, it should be their choice whether or not they want to give birth. Krauthammer also is against capital punishment and would rather have criminals pay for their actions through other ways rather than the death penalty. The fact that Krauthammer has opinions that can be seen on both the right and left side show a grandeur for knowledge and depth in many issues as well as showing above all his desires for the people around him to have a choice in what they believe in. *Things That Matter: Three Decades of Passions, Pastimes and Politics* contains all of Krauthammer's past articles in all of their raw glory with only minor grammatical changes and tiny edits to be rid of typos, redundancy and the occasional obscurity that was found in his articles after they had already been printed in the *Washington Post*. Despite these minor changes, these articles within *Things That Matter* still show how Krauthammer still stands behind what he had previously written and will hold his head high amongst scrutiny. Even though times have changed and ideas are evolving, Krauthammer's original words still prevail and will show in time the ideals of the United States long past its publication. *Things*

That Matter contains over eighty articles, essays, and magazine pieces that are divided into four different sections such as global themes, historical themes, political and his personal thoughts and musings. No piece within the book needs to be read in order, so all readers are free to choose to read whatever may flit their fancy at the time. No matter which article one may choose to read, Krauthammer's writing is so relatable across all ideas that many will find that they will not be able to help but read all of the articles even if they don't agree with what he has to say on a particular subject. There are many types of subjects one may choose to read such as Krauthammer's view on *Time* magazine's choice on Person of the Century being

Albert Einstein, while Krauthammer believes that the award should have gone to Winston Churchill for his total indispensability as well as how his actions are a part of how the world is today. Krauthammer even has views on the idea of using swear words in public such as the F-word and how the Federal Communications Commission once decreed that the use of the F-word could be done as an adjective, but never a verb. Krauthammer is aware that his writings may not be for every reader, however his awareness of his own imperfections is one of the ways that makes his writing perfect in their own way. His articles remain to be compelling, intelligent and thought-provoking no matter what side you take, making him to feel more like a friend rather than a political foe. No matter what you may be feeling on what you want to read, Krauthammer will have an article for you to enjoy.

Discussion Questions

"Get Ready to Enter a New World"

Tip: Begin with questions dealing with broader issues to ensure ample time for quality discussions. Read through all discussion questions before engaging.

~~~

question 1

Krauthammer used to be a member of the Democratic Party, then switched to conservative. How do you think readers will react to that?

~~~

~ ~ ~

question 2

Krauthammer is now more conservative, but still has views that are the opposite. How does that help his cause?

~ ~ ~

~~~

question 3

One of Krauthammer's views is that there should
be free market. What do you think of that idea?

~~~

~~~

question 4

One of Krauthammer's views is that there should be a more limited government. What do you think of that idea?

~~~

~~~

question 5

Krauthammer believes there should be lower taxes.
Do you agree? Why or why not?

~~~

~~~

question 6

Krauthammer is pro-choice when it comes to abortions. Do you agree? Why or why not?

~~~

~~~

question 7

Krauthammer believes there should be stronger individual rights. How do you think that would help people?

~~~

~ ~ ~

question 8

Krauthammer is against capital punishment. Do you think that is valid? Why or why not?

~ ~ ~

~~~

question 9

Krauthammer believes that the Person of the Century should have been Winston Churchill instead of Albert Einstein. What do you think?

~~~

~~~

question 10

Krauthammer admits to using many swear words in public. What are your views on swear words in public?

~~~

~~~

question 11

Krauthammer mentions that being white or being a male is not an attribute these days. Do you think this is valid? Why or why not?

~~~

~~~

question 12

Krauthammer believes that Holocaust will fade from time as generations pass. Do you agree? Why or why not?

~~~

question 13

Krauthammer did not change any of his articles when he published his book. Do you think that is wise? Why or why not?

~~~

question 14

Krauthammer believes that the Angry White Male was invented to rationalize the election of 1994. Do you agree? Why or why not?

~~~

~ ~ ~

question 15

None of Krauthammer's articles need to be read in chronological order. How do you think this will effect readers?

~ ~ ~

~~~

question 16

One reviewer believes that *Things That Matter* should be a required reading. Do you agree? Why or why not?

~~~

~~~

question 17

One reviewer thought that the essays felt as if Krauthammer just had a deadline to hit. What do you think?

~~~

~~~

question 18

One reviewer stated that reading Krauthammer's book will challenge readers due to its diverse intellectual topics. Do you agree? Why or why not?

~~~

~~~

question 19

One reviewer appreciated that Krauthammer did not make them feel lower for having a different opinion in some of his articles. Do you agree? Why or why not?

~~~

~ ~ ~

question 20

One reviewer believed *Things That Matter* to be too opinionated. Do you think this is valid? Why or why not?

~ ~ ~

Introducing the Author

Irving Charles Krauthammer has led an interesting life. He graduated with a BA from McGill University. He graduated in 1970 with First Class Honors in both political science and in economics. Krauthammer decided to study as a Commonwealth Scholar in politics at Balliol College at Oxford University before returning to the United States and continuing his education with an MD at the prestigious Harvard Medical School. Unfortunately during his first year at Harvard while Krauthammer was swimming with friends, he had an accident while diving off of a diving board that ended with his spinal cord being severed and being paralyzed from the waist down. His injury didn't slow him down for long as after fourteen months of recovering from his accident, during which he kept up with his other classmates despite being in the hospital, Krauthammer went back to medical school and eventually graduated to become a psychiatrist. He used his degree and helped create the Diagnostic and Statistical Manual of Mental Disorders III in the year 1980. Krauthammer also joined the Carter administration in 1978 as the director of psychiatric research and soon was acknowledged for his work and became the speechwriter to the Vice President himself, Walter Mondale in 1980. Krauthammer enjoyed writing so much that he decided to make his career revolve around writing his ideas on the world around him. In the late 1970s, he became a political commentator and a columnist. He found a job for *The Washington Post* as a weekly editorial columnist which eventually earned him the Pulitzer Prize for Commentary in 1987 for his columns on national issues. He became so popular that Krauthammer was invited to be a weekly panelist on a PBS program called *Inside Washington* in 1990 and continued that position with pleasure until the news program ceased to be produced in 2013. Krauthammer kept his writing skills up to code and contributed as an editor to *The Weekly Standard*, he became a Fox News Channel contributing guest and he was on a Fox News Channel's show, *Special Report with Bret Baier* as a nightly panelist. Krauthammer continued to be recognized for his writing on foreign policy and received many acclaims for it. He became a leader for the neoconservative group and a proponent of the United Stated political engagement and military on a global scale. Krauthammer advocated for the Iraq War, the Gulf War, enhanced interrogation techniques against suspected terrorists and he coined the term "Reagan Doctrine" during his time spent in the White House. In the year 2013, Krauthammer published *Things That* Matter which contained his articles and essays in one convenient book. His book became an instant bestseller with *The New York* Times and remained in that position for thirty-eight weeks, ten of which had it in the number one spot. Krauthammer loved being a Fox News Contributor, but his ailing health and battle with cancer forced him to stop writing his column and serving the community on the screen in August 2017. Krauthammer eventually succumbed to his cancer and died on June 21, 2018.

Bonus Downloads

*Get Free Books with **Any Purchase** of Conversation Starters!*

Every purchase comes with a FREE download!

Add spice to any conversation
Never run out of things to say
Spend time with those you love

Get it Now

or Click Here.

Scan Your Phone

Fireside Questions

"What would you do?"

Tip: These questions can be a fun exercise as it spurs creativity among the readers by allowing alternate scene endings and "if this was you" questions.

~~~

question 21

Krauthammer went to Oxford University, but changed and went to Harvard instead. How do you think that change contributed to his later life?

~~~

~~~

question 22

Krauthammer broke his spine making him paralyzed. How do you think he felt when that happened?

~~~

~~~

question 23

Krauthammer continued his education while he was in the hospital. How do you think his professors saw his determination?

~~~

~~~

question 24

Krauthammer worked in the White House as the speech writer for the Vice President. How do you think he felt when he received that job?

~~~

question 25

Krauthammer won the Pulitzer Prize for his columns. How do you think he felt when he was nominated to win that prestigious award?

question 26

Krauthammer switched from Oxford University to Harvard including his degree. What do you think would have happened differently if he had stayed in England?

~~~

question 27

Krauthammer is pro-choice for abortions. Do you think he would have changed his mind if someone he loved decided to make a choice? What do you think would be different, if anything?

~~~

question 28

Krauthammer received a spot in *The Washington Post* where he wrote his many articles. What do you think would have happened if he never got that spot?

~~~

question 29

Krauthammer received the Pulitzer Prize for his columns. What do you think would be different if he was never awarded that prize?

~~~

~~~

question 30

Krauthammer died of cancer in 2018. What do you think he would be doing if he was still alive?

~~~

Quiz Questions

"Ready to Announce the Winners?"

Tip: Create a leaderboard and track scores to see who gets the most correct answers. Winners required. Prizes optional.

~~~

quiz question 1

True or False: *Things that Matter* is a compilation of Krauthammer's articles. He wrote them with *The New York Times.*

~~~

~~~

quiz question 2

True or False: Krauthammer began as a democrat. He slowly changed to conservative.

~~~

~~~

quiz question 3

Krauthammer has many ideas on how the government should be run. He believes there should be _____ taxes.

~~~

quiz question 4

Krauthammer isn't fully conservative. He is against _____ when it comes to criminals.

~~~

~~~

quiz question 5

True or False: Krauthammer knows what women go through during a pregnancy. He is pro-choice.

~~~

~~~

quiz question 6

True or False: Krauthammer believes the government does a great job with the country. He is against limited government.

~~~

quiz question 7

Krauthammer has his own ideas on who Person of the Century should be. He believes _____ should have been awarded it.

~~~

quiz question 8

True or False: Krauthammer has earned his degrees. He graduated with in economics and political science for his bachelors.

~~~

~~~

quiz question 9

True or False: Krauthammer broke his spine. He broke it during a skiing accident in England.

~~~

quiz question 10

Krauthammer's writing became well known. He was invited to be the speech writer for the
_____.

~~~

quiz question 11

True or False: Kauthammer was nominated for the Pulitzer Prize. He won in the year 1988.

~~~

~~~

quiz question 12

Krauthammer has done much for this country. He
actually coined the term _____.

~~~

Quiz Answers

1. False
2. True
3. Lower
4. Capital punishment
5. True
6. False
7. Winston Churchill
8. True
9. False
10. Vice President
11. False
12. Reagan doctrine

Ways to Continue Your Reading

EVERY month, our team runs through a wide selection of books to pick the best titles for readers and reading groups, and promotes these titles to our thousands of readers – sometimes with free downloads, sale dates, and additional brochures.

Click here to sign up for these benefits.

If you have not yet read the original work or would like to read it again, you can purchase the original book here.

Bonus Downloads
*Get Free Books with **Any Purchase** of* Conversation Starters!

Every purchase comes with a FREE download!

Add spice to any conversation
Never run out of things to say
Spend time with those you love

Get it Now

or Click Here.

Scan Your Phone

On the Next Page...

If you found this book helpful to your discussions and rate it a 4 or 5, please write us a review on the next page.

Any length would be fine but we'd appreciate hearing you more! We'd be very encouraged.

Till next time,

BookHabits

"Loving Books is Actually a Habit"

CPSIA information can be obtained
at www.ICGtesting.com
Printed in the USA
LVHW051412070620
657613LV00001B/164